THE 30-DAY CREATIVITY CHALLENGE

D1055884

ED BELL

Bell, Ed
Book : The 30-Day Creativity Challenge

Library of Congress Control Number: 2019905747

ISBN 978-0-9981302-4-8 (Paperback edition)

Published June 2019
New York City

CONTENTS

ABOUT THE SONG FOUNDRY

At The Song Foundry it's our mission to share great songwriting ideas with the world. At thesongfoundry.com we publish articles about songwriting, host free videos on various songwriting topics, and offer Skype songwriting coaching worldwide.

Connect with us online to find out more:

thesongfoundry.com

youtube.com/TheSongFoundry

facebook.com/TheSongFoundry

twitter.com/TheSongFoundry

OK, LET'S GET YOUR CREATIVITY ON

Hello. Holá. Konichiwa. And welcome to *The 30-Day Creativity Challenge*, a unique set of daily challenges designed to turn your creative skills up to eleven.

Over the next thirty days you'll find yourself thinking up twenty unusual things you can do with household items, turning bare sketches into interesting images and reflecting on what creativity means more broadly in your life – all with the ultimate goal of making yourself more creative.

But hang on a second. Is that definitely a thing? Is creativity something you can learn?

The short answer is yes. A slightly longer answer is yesss. And an even longer answer is yes – scientists have studied it.* (And artists could have told you it anyway.)

See, just like you'd find it weird if anyone said "I just don't speak French" or "Gosh darn it, I just don't play the clarinet" – as if it's possible to be good those things without trying – there's no such thing as "I'm just not creative."

Instead, there's only "Well, actually, I'm as creative as anyone else, I've just not spent a ton of time developing that particular skill yet."

---

* For an eminently readable summary of some of this research, check out **http://creativityatwork.com/2012/03/23/can-creativity-be-taught/**

In other words: **creativity is not a talent you have, it's a skill you learn**. It's something you get better at the more you do it. It's something you improve by *practicing it.*

And, in short, that's what this book is here to help you do.

The challenges are pretty mixed in what they'll have you do – which means you'll enjoy some more than others, and might find some of them weird or a bit crazy. Well, some of them are weird or a bit crazy. But don't go skipping anything – that's really important.

Because the truth is, the most important thing you need to do in working through these challenges is to get into the habit of working through them – to give yourself the time and space you need to be creative. Because, just like in the gym, developing your creative muscles means putting in your creative reps. Because, as dancer, choreographer and author Twyla Tharp said, "Creativity is a habit, and the best creativity is the result of good work habits."

So before you start, you'll need a plan for setting aside a 15-minute slot every day for thirty days – ten minutes for the challenge, plus a few extra to read and understand it – without fail.

You can do the challenges whenever you like, but for the sake of making them a habit, I recommend you pick the same or a similar time each day. (First thing in the morning – while your mind is still fresh – is a great time.) Then, all you'll need to work through them is a pen or pencil and a pad of paper. Some of the challenges you could do on a phone or tablet, but so you can focus for ten minutes without distractions, writing on something that won't buzz with notifications is a great idea.

Of course, if you're super keen you could do two or even three challenges per day. I recommend doing them over thirty as they were designed, but it's cool if you want to try something different. As long as you carve out thirty uninterrupted 15-minute slots to do the challenges, you'll get all the benefits you can from them.

Finally, each challenge comes with a specific target – like think of at least twenty things that fit some specific criteria, or draw at least fifteen things that do something specific. I based these goals on what's typically possible in ten minutes to give you a target to aim for – but if you do less or more some days, that's OK. As I said, I tried to make the challenges open-ended enough that anyone can do them, so your results may vary, and that's fine.

And that's basically all there is to it.

Since they're creative challenges, there are no right answers – so you won't find any answers at the back of the book. But if you're the kind of person who loves to compare your answers to someone else's, you could find a friend to do the challenges at the same time and then compare notes. (That's also a great way to hold yourself accountable if you know that's going be difficult for you.)

So there we go.

Here's to the art – and skill – of being creative. The art – and skill – of creating something out of nothing. The art – and skill – of not just thinking outside of the box but of realizing there only was a box in the first place if you're happy to put yourself inside one.

And, by the way, it's an art and skill that isn't just for artists and quote-unquote creative people. It's for entrepreneurs who want to solve people's problems. It's for employees who want to be more productive and more engaged at their job. It's for anyone who wants to have better personal relationships, it's for anyone who wants to live a more rewarding, more interesting life, and – best of all – it's for anyone who wants to leave the world a better place than they found it.

It's an art and skill for anyone who wants to be smarter and faster about creating *anything*. Because that's the best thing about creative skills – they apply to *everything* creative. And once you have them, you can have fun using them whenever you like and wherever you like, whatever you decide is worth creating.

Because as Albert Einstein supposedly said, "Creativity is intelligence having fun."

Except, truth be told, he probably didn't – it turns out someone turned 'attributing snappy one liners to famous dead scientists' into their own creative project. But the sentiment is definitely true: creativity is supposed to be fun.

So without further ado, let's go have some.

[DAY 1]
THE BUCKET LIST

[DAY 1]

THE BUCKET LIST

"Creativity involves breaking out of established patterns in
order to look at things in a different way."
EDWARD DE BONO

Lots of people think creativity is just coming up with ideas out of
nothing. And while that's kind of true, all creative ideas have to come
from *somewhere*: they come from things, concepts or ideas that
already exist but get put together in new and unexpected ways.

Your first challenge – thinking up unusual things to do with
everyday items – gives you the opportunity to practice exactly that.

Why it matters: Creativity is about taking existing
concepts and ideas and doing something new with
them.

DAY 1 CHALLENGE

 10 mins

Think of <u>at least twenty things you can do with a bucket</u>.

Remember: you get bonus points for every unusual answer you come up with. So 'watering the plants' is an OK answer. But 'ridiculous paperweight' is a great one.

And as I said in the introduction, if you get to twenty things well before ten minutes is up, keep going.

[DAY 2]
GREEN DAY

[DAY 2]

GREEN DAY

"To have a great idea, have a lot of them."
"When you have exhausted all possibilities, remember this
– you haven't."
THOMAS EDISON

It's easy to assume that great, creative thinkers are just better at coming up with great, creative ideas. But that's not how it works.

Great, creative thinkers have as many terrible ideas as everyone else. They're just better at saying no to their average or OK ideas and pushing themselves to keep trying different things until they get to the really interesting ones.

In other words, creative people are good at coming up with way more ideas than they need – then picking out the best ideas from all the options. That's what today's challenge is all about.

Why it matters: Coming up with your best creative ideas means trying out tons of different ideas, so you can pick out the best ones.

DAY 2 CHALLENGE

 10 mins

Come up with <u>at least forty objects that are green</u>.

It's OK to come up with obvious answers – like 'grass' – especially when you start. But once you've exhausted those, to get to forty objects you'll have to start thinking up not-so-obvious answers too – like 'Teenage Mutant Ninja Turtles'.

Once you're done, take a moment to pick out your best four or five ideas, if you like.

[DAY 3]
ONE-LINERS

[DAY 3]

ONE-LINERS

"But out of limitations comes creativity."
DEBBIE ALLEN

Creativity thrives on limitations. Lots of people assume it's the opposite, but *not* being able to do *anything* helps you focus on doing *something*. And often those limitations help you do that something in a specific and distinctive way you might not have thought of otherwise.

Today's challenge is a drawing challenge with a simple limitation: you can't take your pen or pencil off the paper.

Why it matters: Being able to work within limitations is an essential part of being creative, and a great way of creating something you might not have done otherwise.

DAY 3 CHALLENGE

 10 mins

Sketch each of these six things in a single line – that is, without taking your pen or pencil off the paper:

> **[1] stick man**
>
> **[2] apple**
>
> **[3] skyscraper**
>
> **[4] sunset**
>
> **[5] virus**
>
> **[6] bus stop**

Rough sketches are fine – you don't have tons of time, so you don't have to add tons of detail.

The real challenge here is finding creative ways to celebrate the restriction imposed on you: to make a feature of the places you'd love to take your pen or pencil off the paper but can't. This includes if you make a mistake or draw something you didn't mean to – keep your pen or pencil on the paper and find a way to work with it.

[DAY 4]
TRAVEL PLANS

[DAY 4]

TRAVEL PLANS

"When you can do a common thing in an uncommon way,
you will command the attention of the world."
GEORGE WASHINGTON CARVER

Today's challenge is about getting from A to B – specifically from London to Barcelona. And like the other brainstorming challenges you've done, the challenge is to think beyond the obvious and see where that takes you.

Why it matters: Creativity often begins by exhausting the obvious or well-known possibilities before pushing yourself into the more unusual ones.

DAY 4 CHALLENGE

 10 mins

Come up with <u>at least fifteen ways you could get from London to Barcelona</u>.

As usual, you can start with more obvious ones – like 'fly' or 'hitchhike'. But then try more unusual ones – like 'coach tour' or 'cargo ship'. So it's not just about listing different types of vehicles, but different contexts or situations you could end up travelling between the two cities.

If you need to check where London and Barcelona are on a map before you start, go ahead. But for reference, they're about 700 miles apart, and there's at least 20 miles of sea to cross to get between them.

[DAY 5]
THE CROSSHAIRS
CHALLENGE

[DAY 5]

THE CROSSHAIRS CHALLENGE

"Every new idea is just a mashup or a remix of one or more
previous ideas."
AUSTIN KLEON

One fun kind of creative project is a theme and variations, where you take the essence of an idea or concept and turn it into tons of related but different things.

Today's challenge is an opportunity to practice that – you're going to take the three elements of a simple crosshairs symbol and see what else you can make with them.

Why it matters: Once you know the tools at your disposal, creating different and interesting things means combining or using those tools in different and interesting ways.

DAY 5 CHALLENGE

 10 mins

Sketch at least fifteen different designs made up of a circle and two straight lines. Then give them names or titles, like these:

Crosshairs   **Ferris Wheel**   **Holy Hand Grenade**

The lines can be any length. The circle can be any size. All of those things can touch each other or not. The goal is to think of as many individual designs as you can, then have some fun labeling them.

Like always, if you get to fifteen designs with time to spare, keep going.

[DAY 6]
COUNTRY-LEBRITIES

[DAY 6]

COUNTRY-LEBRITIES

"Creativity is the ability to see relationships where none
existed."
THOMAS DISCH

OK. Let's have some fun.

One of the best things about being creative is that it's not always about coming up with great ideas, but often about discovering great ideas that are already sitting out there somewhere, just waiting to be noticed.

Today's challenge – a fun game of mashing up country and celebrity names – is a chance to do just that: to connect things you already know about in ways you've never thought of before.

> **Why it matters:** Creativity is discovery – it's about making connections between things you already know about, but in unexpected ways.

DAY 6 CHALLENGE

 10 mins

Sometimes, you can mash the end of a country name into the name of a celebrity, like this:

Argentina + Tina Turner = ArgenTina Turner

Sudan + Daniel Radcliffe = SuDaniel Radcliffe

<u>Find at least twelve more of them.</u>

What counts as a country and what counts as a celebrity? Ten minutes isn't enough time to debate whether Taiwan counts as a sovereign nation or how many Twitter followers anyone has. So use your judgment: if most people you know would agree that somewhere is a country or someone is a celebrity, it's all good.

[DAY 7]
THE EMOJI
CHALLENGE

[DAY 7]

THE EMOJI CHALLENGE

"Get into your own creativity. Sketch and paint with
different mediums and follow your heart."
PETER MAX

Yesterday's challenge was about discovering things that fit a specific
format – they either work or they don't. In today's challenge there's
also a specific theme, but you get much more room to use your
imagination and do things your way.

Why it matters: Creativity is about rolling with a
specific idea or theme, then adding your own brand of
imagination and ingenuity to it.

DAY 7 CHALLENGE

 10 mins

Draw fifteen medium-sized circles. Now add lines and shapes to make them into <u>fifteen different emojis expressing different emotions</u>.

This challenge isn't just about replicating the fifteen emojis in your most-used tab. You can make up new ones or reinvent existing ones – just aim to make each one express a different mood or emotion.

[DAY 8]
FREE WRITE #1

[DAY 8]

FREE WRITE #1

"If you hear a voice within you say 'you cannot paint,' then
by all means paint, and that voice will be silenced."
VINCENT VAN GOGH

Sometimes the best and craziest ideas start out as the worst and weirdest ideas. Being creative means being able to silence your inner critic – at least to begin with – so you don't censor any great ideas before they have the opportunity to become great.

That's one of the reasons I don't believe in writer's block. Just like you have to let a tap run for a second to get past the stale and stagnant water, if you just start creating something – anything – the good stuff will flow soon enough.

Today's free writing challenge – a challenge to write for ten minutes without stopping – is a great way to practice that.

Why it matters: Editing and filtering is an important part of the creative process, but early on it's also important to be able to let your ideas flow without changing or rejecting them.

DAY 8 CHALLENGE

 10 mins

Start writing with the following prompt, and keep writing for ten minutes without stopping, editing or filtering yourself:

> **"One day last summer, I ..."**

[DAY 9]
WORD GAPS

[DAY 9]

WORD GAPS

"Make an empty space in any corner of your mind, and
creativity will instantly fill it."
DEE HOCK

Sometimes – like in yesterday's challenge – being creative is about letting your mind wander freely to see where it takes you. But sometimes, creative problems are more specific: they're about working within a bigger vision or idea and filling the gaps between that vision and a finished project.

In fact, starting with a big vision or plan, then filling in smaller and smaller gaps until the project is complete, is a great description of the creative process in general.

Today's challenge is an opportunity to do that in miniature: to see things that aren't there yet and to create your own solutions to fill specific gaps.

Why it matters: Creativity is about looking at what you're creating, figuring out what's missing, then filling those gaps with something that works.

DAY 9 CHALLENGE

 10 mins

Think of <u>at least six words</u> that fill in each of these letter gaps:

     [1] T _ _ T

     [2] D _ _ E

     [3] _ _ _ K _

     [4] _ E T _

     [5] _ _ S _ _

Like always, if you find thirty words before the ten minutes is up, spend the rest of the time finding more.

[DAY 10]
TWENTY PLACES

[DAY 10]

TWENTY PLACES

"Others have seen what is and asked why. I have seen what
could be and asked why not."
PABLO PICASSO

Today you've got your final pure brainstorming challenge. This time,
instead of finding things that fit a particular description, you're going
to be suggesting things that suit a particular purpose.

The challenge is about taking a thing people do maybe once or
twice in their life – proposing – and suggesting different and even
unusual places to do it.

Why it matters: Creativity is all about context and
purpose: what you're doing and why you're doing it.

DAY 10 CHALLENGE

 10 mins

Think of <u>at least twenty creative places someone could propose to their significant other</u>.

The crux of this challenge is understanding what is and isn't a good fit. Exactly what a proposal should be like is a matter of opinion, but given the purpose of most marriage proposals, 'in a sewage works' isn't a great answer. Neither is 'by the Eiffel Tower' – because it's such a clichéd answer.

Try to come up with twenty different places that would be great for a marriage proposal, but that most people would never have considered.

[DAY 11]
WORD HALVES

[DAY 11]

WORD HALVES

"The creation of something new is not accomplished by the
intellect but by the play instinct. The creative mind plays
with the objects it loves."
CARL JUNG

Today you're going to practice one of the most important creative
skills there is: playing around with ideas just to see where your
curiosity takes you.

You've done some similar challenges before, but today you'll get
a lot more freedom to let your mind play – because that's one of the
best ways to come up with your most unusual and unexpected ideas.

Of course, in the end, every creative project has a particular goal
or purpose. But sometimes you have to put that out of your mind
long enough to give yourself some time to play and wonder, just to
see what you discover.

Why it matters: Sometimes, the best way to come up
with your most interesting and innovative ideas is to let
your mind play and wander without any specific purpose
or goal.

DAY 11 CHALLENGE

Take at least fifteen words of two or more syllables or two-word phrases, split them into two parts, then switch each part out for a synonym or related word.

So, for example, 'Guinea pig' (African country – farm animal) could become 'Togo cow'. Or 'paperclip' could become 'cardtag'.

Take whatever words you like, but the goal is to play around – to free associate and see what your brain comes up with. Pick any starting words and phrases that you want – just aim for at least fifteen in ten minutes.

[DAY 12]
THE AUTOGRAPH
CHALLENGE

[DAY 12]

THE AUTOGRAPH CHALLENGE

"In order to be irreplaceable, one must always be different."
COCO CHANEL

Today's challenge is another drawing challenge, but something different: you're going to try drawing something – your signature – as if you were ten different people.

It's an opportunity to imagine ten different lives you might have ended up in, and what autographs those ten different personalities would sign. Being creative is about doing things in your way, to your rules, and this challenge gives you a chance to play around with that.

Why it matters: A big part of being creative is expressing your personality and tastes: who you are, how you think and what makes you tick.

DAY 12 CHALLENGE

 10 mins

Come up with <u>at least ten different ways of signing your name</u> that express ten different personalities.

You can use a pseudonym if you like. Just try to capture ten different personalities in what you create – e.g. formal, fun, crazy, self-important, etc.

[DAY 13]
ASSUMING
OTHERWISE

[DAY 13]

ASSUMING OTHERWISE

"It is important that students bring a certain ragamuffin, barefoot irreverence to their studies; they are not here to worship what is known, but to question it."

JACOB BRONOWSKI

One of the most important things a creative person can do is to question everything. Seriously. It's impossible to create something individual unless you think individually and question the status quo that most people just accept at face value.

That doesn't mean that creative people are always right – and that people who don't question what they told are always wrong – but it does mean that to be an original thinker you have to get used to not following the crowd.

Today's challenge is about questioning assumptions – diving into some simple statements to figure out how true they really are.

Why it matters: Being a creative thinker means questioning what you're told and asking yourself what assumptions you're making before you reach any firm conclusions.

DAY 13 CHALLENGE

 10 mins

Take each of these five statements and <u>list at least three assumptions that have to be true to make the statements true.</u>

[e.g.] <u>The sky is blue...</u>

...except if it's nighttime.

...unless you're on Venus.

...assuming you don't think it's more accurate to describe it as turquoise or cyan.

[1] Grass is green...

[2] It's faster to fly than take the train...

[3] The customer is always right...

[4] You have to spend money to make money...

[5] Everything happens for a reason...

This is an opportunity to play devil's advocate for a second and have fun questioning the kind of assumptions we all make, but that aren't always 100% true.

[DAY 14]
FREE WRITE #2

[DAY 14]

FREE WRITE #2

"Don't think. Thinking is the enemy of creativity. It's self-conscious, and anything self-conscious is lousy. You can't try to do things. You simply must do things."
RAY BRADBURY

Today's challenge is another free write.

By now you know the drill: just keep going. No editing, no filtering, no stopping. Just see where your brain takes you.

This free write goes a bit deeper than the last. Creative people often say they don't write to express what they feel, but they write to *find out* what they think and feel.

So if you look at the prompt and are not sure how to answer it right away – that's great. Just start writing, whatever comes out, and see where you end up ten minutes later.

Why it matters: Sometimes creating something new means leaping into something without knowing what you think or feel about it, then finding that out as you start creating.

DAY 14 CHALLENGE

 10 mins

Start writing with the following prompt, and keep writing for ten minutes without stopping, editing or filtering yourself:

"**If I ran the world, I ...**"

[DAY 15]
THE RELATIONSHIP
CHALLENGE

[DAY 15]

THE RELATIONSHIP CHALLENGE

"I am a part of all that I have met."
ALFRED, LORD TENNYSON

Everything in life – and creativity – is about relationships, context and connections. You are defined by everyone you've ever interacted with. Every part of a creative project is defined by its relationship to the other parts of that creative project.

That means being creative is about being razor sharp about understanding the relationships between people and things – understanding how individual people or things work together (or in opposition) to create something larger than the sum of their parts.

Today's challenge is an opportunity to practice doing that, while finding creative ways to represent those connections on a page.

Why it matters: Thinking creatively means understanding the relationships between individual people and things.

DAY 15 CHALLENGE

 10 mins

<u>Spend ten minutes creating a relationships mind map</u>, starting with you in the center.

A mind map is a visual representation of concepts, ideas and relationships on a page. In this case, start by putting your name in the center of the page and then draw a box round it.

From there, start drawing branches off your name to other significant people in your life. Think not just close friends and family, but work connections, other social connections, former friends, even people you don't really get on with.

As you go, try to find creative ways to represent the direct connections between you and the people in your life, plus any connections between those people outside of their relationship to you. Did your ex and your mom get on really well? Show that on the mind map. Does your mailman hate your dog? Show that too.

There are no rules for how you should represent any individual person or the relationship between them – dotted lines, squiggly lines, colored lines, anything. So invent them. Depending on how many people you know, your map might get messy – and that's OK. The challenge is to see how much of your life you can represent on a single side of paper in ten minutes.

[DAY 16]
THE CIRCLE
CHALLENGE

[DAY 16]

THE CIRCLE CHALLENGE

"Creativity is just connecting things. When you ask creative
people how they did something, they feel a little guilty
because they didn't really do it, they just saw something."
STEVE JOBS

On Day 7 you took fifteen circles and made them fifteen different emojis. Today's challenge is also about drawing circles and turning them into finished images, only now you have the freedom to turn them into anything you like.

Why it matters: Creativity thrives under limitations, but sometimes you get a lot of creative freedom – and an opportunity to have some fun bringing your own vision to a creative project.

DAY 16 CHALLENGE

 10 mins

Draw fifteen circles. <u>Now make them fifteen different things</u> – a tennis ball, planet earth etc. Anything you like.

[DAY 17]
THE EXPLANATION
CHALLENGE

[DAY 17]

THE EXPLANATION CHALLENGE

"Creativity is contagious. Pass it on."
ALBERT EINSTEIN

As fun and worthwhile as it is to do creative challenges just for the sake of it, for a real-world creative project to have meaning beyond itself it has to have some kind of social value. That is, it has to do something for someone else – maybe entertain them, give them information, or make their life easier somehow.

That means part of being creative is communication – being able say what you believe and create what you believe in in a way that affects, helps or just speaks to other people.

Today's challenge is an opportunity to practice doing that.

Why it matters: Creativity is about using your skills, interests and tastes to create something that benefits, entertains or inspires other people.

DAY 17 CHALLENGE

 10 mins

Pick one of these five things:

> **[1] How to iron a shirt**
>
> **[2] How to start a fire**
>
> **[3] How to change your bedding**
>
> **[4] How to change a tire**
>
> **[5] How to make a filter coffee**

<u>Now explain it, step by step, as if you're speaking to a five-year-old.</u>

The key here is to question your assumptions about what you need to include – and to make sure you don't skip over any information that a five-year-old would need to understand.

It's a creative project – so you can do this however you like, with sketches, drawings, anything. But I recommend you aim for maybe four to eight steps, then make each one as simple and clear as possible.

[DAY 18]
THE DRAW-IT-
YOURSELF
RORSCHACH TEST

[DAY 18]

THE DRAW-IT-YOURSELF RORSCHACH TEST

"We adore chaos because we love to produce order."

M. C. ESCHER

You might have heard of the Rorschach test – a psychological test where people are asked to stare at an inkblot and describe what they see. Their answers are supposed to reveal deep insights about their personalities and the way they see the world. Or something.

But since this is a creativity challenge, it's not about interpreting what's there – it's about creating it. You'll get four different starting points to add something imaginative and creative, and then it's up to you share what you see.

You've already done a few drawing challenges, but by focusing on only four images, today you can enjoy creating something more detailed and substantial.

Why it matters: Creativity is about taking what's already there and doing your own thing with it.

DAY 18 CHALLENGE

⏱ **10 mins**

Copy out these four skeleton sketches and add to them to create <u>four completed, specific images</u>.

The final images can be anything you like – yes, anything – but you get bonus points if they suggest some kind of story, situation or action. For example, you could make a triangle a piece of cheese that someone is grabbing, or a ramp a kid on a skateboard is about to jump off. You have time to add some detail to each image.

You can rotate or flip the skeleton sketches if you like, just don't take away any of the lines that are already there.

[1]   **[2]**

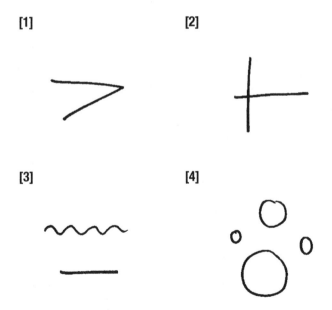

[3]   **[4]**

[DAY 19]
FREE WRITE #3

[DAY 19]

FREE WRITE #3

"Inspiration is for amateurs.
The rest of us just show up and get to work."
CHUCK CLOSE

Today's challenge is your third and final free write. In the previous two you wrote directly from your personal perspective. This time you're writing about someone else.

You'll get a prompt, like before, then it's over to you to write whatever comes to mind. As always, the trick is not to stop, reflect, edit or censor yourself – just take the prompt, let it flow and see where it takes you.

Why it matters: Free writing is about practicing getting yourself into a state where you let your ideas flow, without filtering or questioning them.

DAY 19 CHALLENGE

 10 mins

Start with the following prompt, and keep writing for ten minutes without stopping, editing or filtering yourself:

"She'd never done this before, but ..."

[DAY 20]
THE EMPATHY
CHALLENGE

[DAY 20]

THE EMPATHY CHALLENGE

"Creativity comes from looking for the unexpected and
stepping outside your own experience."

MASARU IBUKA

Since so much in creativity comes down to personal opinion and preference, creative people tend to be really good at recognizing that their point of view isn't the only point of view. They understand that everyone has their own perspectives and values, and (most of the time) these are as valid as anyone else's.

On Day 29, I'll challenge you to get behind something you strongly believe in, but today is your chance to do that for other people: to think about people you completely disagree with and consider why their perspective is valid even if it's totally different from yours.

> **Why it matters:** A cornerstone of creativity is being able to see things from other people's perspectives, whether you agree with them or not.

DAY 20 CHALLENGE

 10 mins

Think of three people you fundamentally disagree with – or have disagreed with in the past. <u>Write around 50–100 words explaining each of their worldviews from their perspectives.</u>

[DAY 21]
THE HEXOMINO
CHALLENGE

[DAY 21]

THE HEXOMINO CHALLENGE

"The world is not limited by IQ.
We are all limited by bravery and creativity."
ASTRO TELLER

Most creative challenges are a mix of creative – where anything goes – and logical – where some things work and some, well, don't.

Today's challenge is a more logical one – you'll get a set of parameters with a limited number of solutions, and it's up to you to find as many of them as you can.

Why it matters: Sometimes you realize that a creative problem has a limited number of solutions, but it's still worth finding as many different ones as possible.

DAY 21 CHALLENGE

 10 mins

A hexomino is a shape made out of six squares joined together edge to edge. Like this:

Or this:

There are thirty-five hexominos in total. **Find at least twenty of them.**

Watch out for any hexominos that are rotations or reflections of the ones you already have, like these, which you can create by rotating or flipping the two hexominos above:

[DAY 22]
THE NEW BUCKET LIST

[DAY 22]

THE NEW BUCKET LIST

"Blessed are the curious, for they shall have adventures."
LOVELLE DRACHMAN

In the introduction I said that in the final few challenges you'd spend some time thinking about what creativity means in your life more broadly. Today is the first of those challenges.

Creating something new is about trying things you've never done before. Because the solution to a problem you've never solved before is almost always a thing you've never done before.

Because you learn best from experience, learning means being open to experiencing new things and putting yourself in unfamiliar places and situations. But a lot of people don't – they stick firmly within their comfort zone. And while comfort zones can be nice places, as the saying goes, nothing interesting grows there.

Breaking out of yours is what today's challenge is about.

Why it matters: Being creative means being open to trying things you've never done before.

DAY 22 CHALLENGE

 10 mins

Come up with <u>at least twenty things you've never done before that you've never really thought about doing until now.</u>

So this isn't just your bucket list – a list of things you want to do before you die that you might have had for ages. It's an opportunity to think of things maybe you *should* want to do before you die – things you know about, you've just never considered could be for you. I don't know: parasailing, visiting Ecuador, running for president – whatever you can think of.

Whether you actually do these things or not is up to you. (Though some of them might be fun, no?) But the real challenge here is to come up with things that you've never seriously thought about doing before – things that are way outside of your go-to hobbies or usual routine.

[DAY 23]
YES WE CAN: PROBLEM SOLVING #1

[DAY 23]

YES WE CAN: PROBLEM SOLVING #1

"The important thing for you is to be alert, to question, to
find out, so that your own initiative may be awakened."

BRUCE LEE

Creativity is about saying 'yes, and…' not 'no, but…'. It's about thinking of ways you can work with the ideas you've got and not shoot them down before you've had chance to play with them. (As you know by now, sometimes the best ideas sound crazy or impossible at first.)

Depending on your outlook, it can take a bit of practice to train yourself to learn to say 'yes, and…' more than anything else. That's what today's challenge is about.

Why it matters: Creativity is about solving problems by saying 'yes', and not shutting down an idea before it's had chance to grow into something amazing.

DAY 23 CHALLENGE 10 mins

Think of your brain as two halves – one that focuses on what's possible and one that thinks lots of things aren't. <u>Continue this conversation between your 'Yes' and 'No' brains for at least fifteen more lines.</u>

> Y: We need to get gas.
>
> N: You don't have cash.
>
> Y: I'll pay with a card.
>
> N: But what if the gas station is closed?
>
> Y: We'll go to another one.
>
> N: But ...

You can take this conversation anywhere you like, but the game is to have your 'No' brain point out everything that could possibly go wrong while your 'Yes' brain finds solutions.

The solutions could be simple or complex, obvious or not. The challenge is to focus on finding solutions to every potential problem that comes up.

[DAY 24]
THREE HAIKUS

[DAY 24]

THREE HAIKUS

"Making the simple complicated is commonplace;
making the complicated simple, awesomely simple,
that's creativity."
CHARLES MINGUS

You've probably heard of haikus – a Japanese poetic form consisting of three lines of five, seven and five syllables. Well, today's challenge is to write three of them.

One of the most fun things about writing haikus is that having only seventeen syllables to play with really challenges you to write compactly and make every single word choice count.

Oh, and in case you've written haikus before and want to make things even more interesting – today's challenge comes with an optional twist.

Why it matters: Simplicity – the art of condensing your ideas into the simplest, most compact, most concentrated form possible – is a key creative skill.

DAY 24 CHALLENGE

 10 mins

Pick three of the following subjects:

[1] **Trees (H)**

[2] **Travel (A)**

[3] **Happiness (I)**

[4] **Pizza (K)**

[5] **The meaning of life (U)**

Now write three haikus – short poems of three lines of five, seven and five syllables – on those subjects.

And if you're already a haiku pro and want an extra challenge: write each haiku without using the bracketed letter after the subject. (So if you chose 'trees', write whatever you like without using the letter 'H'.)

The trick with writing great haikus is not just fitting a specific syllable count but writing words that fit the form *and* have their own meaning or impact. So try writing something that's funny, moving or thought-provoking in some way, that just seems to fit the particular syllable pattern. (Even if it took work to make it seem that way.)

If you finish way before the ten minutes is up, go back and see if you can tweak or improve what you've got.

[DAY 25]
THE FAILURE
CHALLENGE

[DAY 25]

THE FAILURE CHALLENGE

"I've learnt so much from my mistakes, I'm thinking of
making a few more."
ANONYMOUS

Don't take this the wrong way, but in today's challenge you're going to reflect on the times you've screwed up.

Because here's the thing: being creative means taking risks. Creating something original means doing something nobody's done before. Which means you have to figure out how. Which means there's a chance you'll never completely figure out how. You can't play it safe *and* innovate. You can't be courageous *and* comfortable. You can't win big without the risk of failing big.

But there's good news: failure isn't really failure. It's a chance to learn something new. It's a chance to improve something. Every time you take a risk you're rewarded: either with what you want or with an important lesson. Today you're going to reflect on that.

Why it matters: Creative people are comfortable taking risks and experiencing failure because they know it's the only way to create something truly remarkable.

DAY 25 CHALLENGE

 10 mins

Think of five times in your life things didn't turn out the way you wanted them to. <u>List them, along with a sentence or two about what those experiences taught you – or how, with hindsight, they helped you grow.</u>

They can be any time things went wrong or that you shot and missed – jobs you didn't get, relationships that broke down, projects that didn't go where you hoped they would. Then ask yourself what you took away from those experiences, even if it wasn't what you wanted at the time.

With hindsight you often realize that the only way to get where you are today was via all the experiences that led you here, screw-ups included. So genuinely, ask yourself what you know or have today you wouldn't know or have if you hadn't experienced what you did.

This is about reprogramming yourself to see failure not just as part of life, but as an inevitable part of trying new things and an *essential* part of growing as a person.

[DAY 26]
THE
STORYBOARDING
CHALLENGE

[DAY 26]

THE STORYBOARDING CHALLENGE

"Don't be too timid and squeamish about your actions.
All life is an experiment. The more experiments you make
the better."
RALPH WALDO EMERSON

Stories are at the heart of being human. They're how we understand the world and our place in it.

Creating stories is also a fun creative challenge, because it tests not only your imagination but your understanding of how people work, what they want, what's stopping them getting it, and how they succeed or fail in achieving their goals.

Today's challenge gives you the opportunity to practice doing all of that, while crafting a series of events into some kind of logical and meaningful order.

Why it matters: Creativity is about connecting the dots in an interesting but logical, meaningful way.

DAY 26 CHALLENGE

 10 mins

Storyboard an adventure of at least fifteen plot points given this start:

> **[1] 7:16am: Mr. Hernandez realized he was out of coffee.**

Generally, you're going to want to make each plot point just one sentence. Your adventure can be sensible, ridiculous or a combination of the two, but the real challenge here is to think about how each plot point connects to the next one – or to others in a different part of the story – with some kind of logic or progression.

In other words, while you can connect consecutive plot points with a sense of 'and' or 'then', your story will be a lot more compelling if you connect most of the plot points with a sense of 'so' or 'but'.

So ask yourself 'what next, and why?' after each plot point and see where that takes you.

You can go back and make changes or edits to the plot points as you create. Fifteen plot points is a great target, but as you know, you're welcome to add more if you get there before ten minutes is up.

[DAY 27]
THE PERSISTENCE
CHALLENGE

[DAY 27]

THE PERSISTENCE CHALLENGE

"When you're going through hell, keep going."
WINSTON CHURCHILL

Creating new things is hard. Sometimes it flows, just like that. But sometimes you rest your mind against a creative problem for hours, days, even months before you get that light bulb moment when everything just clicks.

But as Louis Pasteur said, "Fortune favors the prepared mind." In other words: creative breakthroughs don't happen purely by chance. The 'aha' moment you get when you see the apple fall from the tree doesn't happen without spending hours and hours before then mulling over how gravity might work.

At least half of success in creativity is persistence: how willing you are to keep going, to hold on for that breakthrough, no matter what. Today's challenge is something different – and while it won't seriously stretch your imagination or intellect, it will definitely test your ability stick things out when they get tough.

Why it matters: Creative ideas don't always flow right away, so persistence is essential in creativity.

DAY 27 CHALLENGE

 10 mins

If you draw five points in a pentagon shape, like this:

You can then use four lines to join all five points together in tons of different ways, like these:

<u>**Draw out as many as you can in ten minutes.**</u> **And oh, here's the crazy part: before you begin, <u>raise your non-writing hand as high as you can and hold it there</u>. If you drop it down, stop the challenge.**

Full disclosure: there are 125 permutations here, including rotations and reflections. So you won't find every single one in ten minutes – even if you can keep your hand up that long – and that's fine. That's the point.

This challenge is hard and it is going to hurt. Your goal is to see how long you can keep going, even when it does.

[DAY 28]
NOT A OR B, BUT C: PROBLEM SOLVING #2

[DAY 28]

NOT A OR B, BUT C: PROBLEM SOLVING #2

"Problems cannot be solved by the same level of thinking
that created them."
ALBERT EINSTEIN

Some of the best creativity comes out of conflict. Maybe you're trying to pull off three things at once. Maybe you're collaborating with someone who wants to do one thing while you try and do something else.

Learning to solve these kinds of problems is a really important part of being creative. And the solutions often come from a really important principle: when it feels like you're stuck between two non-ideal options, you usually aren't. There's nearly always a third, fourth or even fifth solution that works all round. Finding these is what today's challenge is all about.

Why it matters: Being creative often means searching that extra bit harder to find a solution that satisfies as many people or perspectives as possible.

DAY 28 CHALLENGE

 10 mins

Solve each of these problems in way that works for both sides:

[1] You want to order in Chinese food but your significant other wants a curry.

[2] Your friend is warm and wants to open a window but you're too cold.

[3] We're going to the store together and you want to bike there because it's better for the environment, but I already worked out today so I'd rather drive.

[4] You want to go out to see an action movie with your significant other Friday night but they're too tired.

[5] Your friend wants to take a trip with you to Madrid to practice her Spanish but you can't afford it.

[6] You decide you and your significant other should go vegetarian for ethical reasons, but they don't want to because they like the taste of meat too much.

[7] Your significant other wants to spend more time apart but you don't. (Invent some motivations here.)

Naturally, this is a creative challenge – so you can solve each problem any way that you can. The key is to try to understand what's motivating each side then finding a way to accommodate both.

If you whizz through each problem in way under ten minutes, keep going: see if you can find alternative solutions that work.

[DAY 29]
THE CORE BELIEFS CHALLENGE

[DAY 29]

THE CORE BELIEFS CHALLENGE

"Great things are not accomplished by those who yield to
trends and fads and popular opinion."
JACK KEROUAC

Being creative often means being a visionary and standing out from
the crowd. That might sound easy, but standing by what you think
when you're surrounded by people who disagree can be tough.

So a big part of being creative is learning to trust your gut and
stick to your values even if it feels like nobody gets you. George
Bernard Shaw said "All great truths begin as blasphemies" –
remember when everyone thought the earth was flat? – so it's
important to be able to stand behind your unconventional ideas and
the values and beliefs that inspired them.

Why it matters: Being creative means learning when
and how to stand your ground, even when most people
disagree with you.

DAY 29 CHALLENGE

🕐 **10 mins**

List three core beliefs you hold that very few other people do. Explain those beliefs in 40–80 words each.

These beliefs can be about anything or anyone. They can be really deep or pretty inconsequential. They can be things you've shared with other people or things you haven't. They could be something like "_____ is massively underrated" or "_____ isn't really wrong" or "_____ is an amazing opportunity that nobody is taking".

If this takes you some time, or is something you need to think about, that's fine. There's no rush to get anything down, or express it in a particularly fancy way. The most important part of this challenge is that you settle on three beliefs, big or small, that make you different from most people.

(Oh, and if you're someone who isn't sure whether you're that different from most people, you categorically, 100% are. Keep digging. You'll find something soon enough.)

[DAY 30]
THE TOP ROW
CHALLENGE

[DAY 30]

THE TOP ROW CHALLENGE

"The world always seems brighter when you've just made
something that wasn't there before."

NEIL GAIMAN

Alrighty: it's time for the big finish. Your final challenge is an opportunity to bring everything you've worked on in the last twenty-nine challenges together in one place.

This challenge will give you the most freedom you've had so far – but also one of the strictest limitations. As always, your goal is to use the freedom and limitations you have to rustle up something interesting that has at least a touch of your unique creative magic.

> **Why it matters:** Creativity is about working with whatever you've got – finding inspiration within your limitations and creating your best, most interesting and most distinctive work, however you can.

DAY 30 CHALLENGE 10 mins

Create something – anything – using only the letters of the top row of a standard US computer keyboard:

Q W E R T Y U I O P

Seriously – create what you like. A poem, a short story, a sketch of the Taj Mahal made of two hundred letter Qs – anything.

Use any kind of punctuation you like. Mix lowercase and uppercase letters as you like, in any style of handwriting or typography you like. Feel free to add lines or shapes or other graphic elements if you want to. Just make sure the only letters you use are the ten above.

Other than that, the world – and the blank page – is your oyster.

THAT'S A WRAP — WHAT NOW?

THAT'S A WRAP – WHAT NOW?

Congratulations – that's a wrap! As well as all the interesting stuff you created, you managed to set aside thirty uninterrupted time slots to work your way through these challenges, and that's no small achievement in itself.

So what happens now?

Well, I wish I could tell you there's a *The 30-Day Creativity Challenge 2: The Re-Createning*, but there's not. (At least, not yet.)

But – as I said in the introduction – there *is* a real world full of opportunities to see things differently, do things differently and leave your personal creative fingerprint on everything you touch.

So over to you.

Try new things. Try mixing things up at home, work and in your free time. Look for opportunities in your life to identify and solve real-life problems. Look for ways to do things differently, do things your own way, or just pursue more of the things that interest you.

But most of all – stay curious. Expose yourself to new people and new ideas. Go to galleries, festivals and museums. Keep reading new things. Share your ideas with other people and seek out the opinions of the people you admire. Spend time alone so you can think without distractions. Do all those things you've never done before – yoga, skydiving, that trip to Ecuador – just to see what happens.

If you're looking for more inspiration, at the end of the book I've included eleven great quotations about creativity that didn't fit anywhere else but were too good not to share with you. There's also a short list of books that you'll enjoy if you want to know more about how creativity works and how you can become even more creative.

Otherwise, all that's left to say is good luck.

The future belongs to those who create it — have fun creating yours.

MORE INSPIRATION

A lot of smart people have said a lot of smart things about creativity. So when I was researching great quotations to contextualize each challenge, I found way more than I ever could have used on thirty of them. (Just like I've encouraged you to do.)

So, of all of the quotations I couldn't find a home for, here are eleven that do such a great job of capturing what it means to be creative that I really wanted to share them with you anyway. Enjoy.

"Creativity is based on the belief that there's no particular virtue in doing things the way they've always been done."
RUDOLPH FLESCH

"You can't use up creativity.
The more you use, the more you have."
MAYA ANGELOU

"It had long since come to my attention that people of accomplishment rarely sat back and let things happen to them. They went out and happened to things."
LEONARDO DA VINCI

"Do not go where the path may lead, go instead where there is no path and leave a trail."
RALPH WALDO EMERSON

"If you are not willing to risk the unusual, you will have to settle for the ordinary."
JIM ROHN

"Only those who will risk going too far can possibly find out how far one can go."
T. S. ELIOT

"Remember the two benefits of failure. First, if you do fail, you learn what doesn't work; and second, the failure gives you the opportunity to try a new approach."
ROGER VON OECH

"Trust your own instinct. Your mistakes might as well be your own, instead of someone else's."
BILLY WILDER

"When all think alike, then no one is thinking."
WALTER LIPPMAN

"The most courageous act is still to think for yourself. Aloud."
COCO CHANEL

"An idea that is not dangerous is unworthy of being called an idea at all."
OSCAR WILDE

MORE TO READ

If you want to become more creative and understand more about how creativity works, these five resources are definitely worth checking out.

Austin Kleon: *Steal Like an Artist*, (Workman, 2012)

> Austin Kleon's classic, *Steal Like an Artist* explores ten fundamental ideas about how creativity works and is a must read for anyone interested in living a more creative life.

Jessica Hagy: *How to Be Interesting*, (Workman, 2013)

> Jessica Hagy's *How to Be Interesting* outlines ten important and actionable steps to make your life more interesting and more creative.

Seth Godin: *The Purple Cow*, (Portfolio, 2009)

> Seth Godin, entrepreneur extraordinaire, explains why in the twenty-first century, it has never been more important to make things that stand out.

Twyla Tharp: *The Creative Habit*, (Simon & Schuster, 2003)

> Twyla Tharp is a celebrated choreographer and artist and her classic book *The Creative Habit* dismantles many of the common myths about how creativity works and outlines how you can make your own life more creative.

Ed Catmull: *Creativity, Inc.*, (Random House, 2014)

> Ed Catmull is President of Pixar and Disney Animation, so he knows a thing or two about creativity and creative collaboration. *Creativity, Inc.* is a unique inside look into the life-changing creative lessons he's learnt over the years.

For more titles, you can also check out my recommended reading at **thesongfoundry.com/bookshelf**.

MORE FOR SONGWRITERS

If you picked up this book as a songwriter and are new to my work as an author, songwriting coach and educator, then there's a ton of fun stuff for you to discover.

There are three more 30-Day Challenges, specifically for songwriters, that will help you improve your lyric writing skills, music composition skills and your ability to write songs quickly and freely.

The Art of Songwriting is a longer book that dives deep into how songs work, how to write your own and what it means to be an artist.

You can check out both of these books – plus tons of free articles, downloads and videos – at **thesongfoundry.com**.